Revolutionary Witticisms of Colin Fox, Rosie Kane and Carolyn Leckie MSPs

Introduced and edited by Gregor Gall

D1396078

Word Power Books

First published in the United Kingdom in 2004 by
Word Power Books
43 West Nicolson Street
Edinburgh
EH8 9DB
www.word-power.co.uk

Cover photographs by Ally Black and *Scottish Socialist Voice*.

ISBN 0-9549185-0-9

Typeset by John Saunders Design & Production
Printed by Biddles Ltd., King's Lynn

About the Editor

Dr Gregor Gall is Professor of Industrial Relations at the University of Stirling. He has written and researched on industrial relations and trade unionism. He is the author of *The Meaning of Militancy? Postal workers and industrial relations* (Ashgate, 2003), *The Political Economy of Scotland: Radical Scotland? Red Scotland?* (University of Wales Press, 2005) and editor of *Union Organising: Campaigning for trade union recognition* (Routledge, 2003) and *Union Recognition: Organising and Bargaining Outcomes* (Routledge, 2005). Forthcoming books are *Tommy Sheridan – a political biography* (University of Wales Press, 2006) and *The Scottish Socialist Party – the development of a new political force* (Welsh Academic Press, 2007). He is also a regular contributor to *Scottish Left Review*, *Frontline*, *Perspectives*, *Scottish Socialist Voice* and *Solidarity* amongst others as well as to newspapers and radio programmes in Scotland and Britain.

Contents

Chapter 1

Introduction: Critical Politics, Critical Humour

Politics in Britain is generally seen as a dry and dull, if worthy and necessary, social process carried out by a small political elite, separate and distant from the mass of ordinary people and even those that vote. Sometimes the subject matter appears to concern the mass of people's ordinary lives but most often it appears irrelevant to their daily lives. At worst, politics is seen as the process of a minority feathering their own nests and those of their ilk. This leads to resignation and alienation from politics, not mobilisation and participation in politics.

Devolution in Scotland has not changed this. The Scottish Parliament appears to be no closer to 'the people' than politics was before 1999, and most see Holyrood as a glorified town council. Indeed, the cost of the parliament building and debates on dog pooh and pigeon control have accentuated this gap, bringing with them even greater scepticism and cynicism about the political process.

Into this malaise within Scotland, and as a result of the 2003 Scottish Parliamentary elections, a number of colourful characters have been inserted into Scottish political life. Prime amongst these are three of the Scottish Socialist Party's new batch of MSPs, namely,

Colin Fox, Rosie Kane and Carolyn Leckie. By their own words and deeds, they offer the prospect of not only livening up the political process in Scotland but also making it a little more relevant to the concerns of ordinary people. Rosie, for example, claims to put the 'fun' and the 'mental' into fundamentalism in politics.

As Scottish Socialist Party (SSP) MSPs, they have pledged to carry the concerns and issues of ordinary people into the Parliament. They have also pledged to use their high profile and colourful and flamboyant personal style of political *modus operandi* to provide a platform for these concerns in society through the media and popular campaigns. All three MSPs use humour and witticisms to convey their messages and tasks, whether attacking the opposition in Parliament or the rich and privileged outside it, or rallying support to their own party and causes. Although the three are not just parliamentarians *per se*, their standing is enhanced by the absence of comparable parliamentarians at Westminster. Some MPs may be humorous individuals but this is not part of their political repertoire. All three also speak in the vernacular of the Scottish tongue, or more precisely, the working class west of Scotland tongue. This has brought difficulties for the official recorders of the Parliament, the equivalent of *Hansard*, but the three have not relented. They believe they should continue to speak as they have done before and as the majority of Scots do outside Parliament.

Whilst the left has traditionally had a reputation for being dull and/or using flowery language to exaggerate, humour has never played a great part in its lan-

guage and mindset. The SSP MSPs use humour and witticisms in an eloquent and spontaneous, but also gen-
uine and populist manner to try to bridge the gap
between official politics and everyday politics with
regard to pursuing socialist and radical causes. They
have brought the sharp wit of 'the street' into official
politics and politics *per se* in order to speak in a language and in a manner that ordinary people can relate
to. This reflects both a conscious strategy as well as the
nature of the individuals themselves. In particular, the
MSPs see that cultural mechanisms of disseminating
political messages are as important as the stock-in-trade
of political meetings and socialist newspapers. No other
similarly colourful and witty characters with high-profile public personae, and particularly on the left, exist.
Hopefully, Colin, Carolyn and Rosie can start to help fill
this yawning gap. Maybe, they can set an example to
others. Their use of humour in a matter-of-fact, down-
to-earth and everyday populist manner may even help
begin the process of creating a counter-culture, indeed,
a popular radical culture which occupies a significant
social space in society in Scotland.

And why no mention of 'The Great Socialist Leader',
Chairman Sheridan, you may rightly ask? Sir Thomas of
Sheridan is seen by some political foes to be devoid of
humour, even soulless. This is not the reason for his
exclusion from the pantheon of revolutionary witticisms
in contemporary Scotland. From a random sample from
the last decade or so, we have the following:

On Glasgow's New Found Status as a City of Culture

> Never mind the Pavarotti. Whit about the Poveratti? (1992)

On Overseas Housing Trips by Labour Councillors when a Councillor Himself

> Maybe there should be trips to log cabins in Drumchapel and wigwams in Easterhouse. (1995)

On the Labour Party Investigation into Labour Councillors' Junkets

> I'm surprised Billy Smart hasn't been appointed because the whole fiasco has turned into a circus. (1997)

On New Labour Policy Initiatives

> It disnae matter how many times you reheat mince. It's still mince. (1999)

On East-West Relations

> Many on the east coast like to think that weegies are soapdodgers. Nothing could be further from the case as Rosie and I visited the workers' picketline at the Soapworks factory in Glasgow. (2004)

So, there is some evidence of humour and witticism in his political activity. Rather, the reason for Tommy's exclusion is that, maybe inclined by the sensibilities of leadership under the spotlight, he uses such humorous linguistic devices far less as part of his political repertoire.

The purpose of this edited collection is several-fold. First, to bring together these witticisms into one collection where only a relatively small number of people may have come across *some* of them before, those being the regular readers of the *Herald* and *Scotsman*. *Revolutionary Witticisms*, therefore, offers a singular source of these witticisms. Second, to bring these witticisms to a wider array of readers than those who read the *Herald* and *Scotsman*, including many who do not read newspapers at all. This would include a younger generation of people who have bought books on anti-globalisation, anti-imperialism and anti-neoliberalism. Third, to try to establish a wider audience for radical politics that does not involve reading dense political tracts. This is to try to go beyond the 'chattering classes' without being a party political (i.e. SSP) project. Finally, to try to insert a necessary element of 'colour' and 'fun' into contemporary Scottish politics by establishing a Scottish dimension to the anti-establishment political humour and political lampooning and satire which is currently popular in Britain. Here, we can recall the popularity and critical acclaim of a substantial number of works: Michael Moore's books (*Downsize This!, TV Nation, Hey Dude, Where's My Country?, Stupid White Men*); Rory Bremner's television series; the Bush-isms book series edited by Jacob Weisberg (*George W. Bushisms, More George W. Bushisms, Still More George W. Bushisms, Ultimate Bushisms*); Jeremy Hardy's radio series (*Jeremy Hardy Speaks to the Nation*); Alistair Beaton's *The Little Book of New Labour Bollocks*; Mark Thomas' various television series (e.g. *The Mark*

Thomas Comedy Product), and Mark Steel's radio series and his books *It's Not A Runner Bean, Reasons to be Cheerful* and *Vive La Revolution*. Before this recent crop, we can remember *Spitting Image*, Ben Elton and Alexi Sayle, Jo Brand and Victoria Wood.

To be sure of avoiding any 'misunderestimation' à la George W. Bush of what a witticism is, what it can do and the potential power of witticisms, a witticism is defined by various dictionaries and thesauruses as:

- clever or witty remark (*Collins' English Dictionary*)
- quip, sally, pun, one-liner (slang), riposte (*Collins' Thesaurus*)
- repartee, wisecrack, epigram (*Chambers' Thesaurus*)
- wittily amusing remark, a sparklingly clever joke (*The New Shorter Oxford English Dictionary*)

The origin of the term, witticism, is derived from the word, witty, and was coined by English poet, dramatist and critic John Dryden (1631-1700) in 1677 by using the word, witty, and making an analogy with the word and term, criticism.

But what makes the witticisms of Colin, Carolyn and Rosie qualify as revolutionary witticisms? Before answering this, I am with a reasonable amount of certainty taking what I consider to pass as their offerings of witticisms as attestable witticisms. Indeed, the diarists and parliamentary sketch writers of the *Herald* and *Scotsman*, amongst others, would concur here. It is not contentious to state that the three MSPs' witticisms, when set in the full and proper context of where and when they were made, are variously leftwing, radical, oppositional, militant and progressive. They are always, at the very least, irreverent and mocking of their political opponents.

But this does not make them revolutionary. What is and is not revolutionary is not always immediately apparent. Sometimes a demand or statement is an explicit clarion call of revolutionary implications, or, of revolution itself. Sometimes such a demand or statement is implicitly revolutionary because it cannot be obtained or accommodated within existing society as we know it. This might be termed as being of a transitional method of taking immediate and far-reaching reforms as a means of building the social forces for revolution. I would suggest that because the commitment of Colin, Carolyn and Rosie to socialism and revolution is deep-seated and firmly held, their witticisms should be seen in this light. Their context and intention are thus important to understanding the individual witticism and to seeing it as part of a bigger canvass on which they paint. And besides, some of the witticisms are just plain amusing and enjoyable. Indeed, using the title 'Revolutionary Witticisms' conveys in an easy and snappy way what the book is broadly about.

Chapter 2

Humour in Politics, Politics as Humour: Interview with Mark Steel

Mark Steel is a popular, high-profile left-wing and subversive comedian and commentator. This interview was conducted in September 2004.

Gregor Gall (GG): Sometimes politics is seen by people as a serious business and, therefore, should not be treated in a light-hearted manner. Could you say what you think the role of humour in politics is?

Mark Steel (MS): In this country, there's a confusion about what politics is and what humour is. Politics is seen to be something that's done by politicians and takes places in the politics pages of newspapers and on the news on television and radio. That's why it seems to have little or no bearing on the lives of ordinary people. The connection that politicians used to have with people has eroded with the collapse in membership of political parties and their presence in communities. But if people in their local pub had an argument about racism, cuts in their local hospital or the Iraq war, they probably wouldn't think that they were doing anything political. This is also probably true of the majority that went on the big anti-war demonstrations in 2002.

It depresses me that some people think that comedy is a sugary way of coating politics for the consumption of ordinary people. Can comedians be funny about serious issues like the Iraq war? This is a ridiculous question because you'd never ask a playwright if they could write a play about the Iraq war. It assumes that comedy can only be funny if it's frivolous and about things that are frivolous. Of course, comedy can deal with serious issues like the Twin Towers. So comedy and humour have an important role to play as long as you recognise that politics is something that affects everybody on a daily basis and that comedy is a legitimate way of looking at the world – just as music and theatre can look at the world. Comedy has to be about something and it can be about the way society is presently run and about whether there is an alternative to this. If you see politics as being about ordinary people's lives then, of course, comedy can be political and almost always is political.

GG: Where do you think the ability of some people to be humorous in politics comes from?

MS: I suppose that it's quite an instinctive thing, although that's not to say that gags and lines can't be worked up and polished. But on the other hand, if you look at *The Life of Brian*, that took time and effort. You can't insert comedy into politics like adding an egg to a cake mix and hope that you end up having a great big cake as a result. I saw Jack Straw giving a speech at a Labour Party conference a few years ago. He must of thought, 'I must inject a bit of humour into politics so I'll do a joke'. Someone had scripted a gag into the opening of his speech for him. It went something like this: 'I'm very pleased that my Cabinet colleague, Lord Sainsbury, the minister for science and technology, has developed a carrot that doubles as a stick'. It fell so flat that he had to fall back on an old politician's joke about not being recognised. That one fell flat too before the delegates realised they were expected to be laughing. That was a travesty for comedy.

Comedy is a way of looking at things. It's a way of seeing the world. For example, when there was a bomb in Casablanca which killed a couple of people several years ago, I was going into the BBC that morning and I said to them in the office: 'I bet you all thought the same thing as I did – the barman looks up from the bar and sees the suicide bomber and says, 'Of all the bars in all the towns, you had to come into mine!' They said in shock and horror 'Of course, we didn't!' and 'How could you?'

GG: Why is politics in Britain so apparently humourless?

MS: The people that object to comedy in politics and political comedy are those who have a certain view about politics. They only object to it when it goes against the mainstream and the establishment. They don't see politics in comedy when it reflects the *status quo*. They only see politics in comedy when it starts attacking the *status quo*. Sometimes they don't see it when it's there and it is attacking the *status quo* like *The Office*. *The Office* is intensely political at one level, making management out to be a bunch of petty minded bosses trying to justify their own existence. On another level, it's about the daily drudgery in people's lives where people live to work and don't work to live. Indeed, most mainstream culture is now at odds with the rules that govern society. For example, most people don't believe that making profits should come before anything else.

I suspect that Charles Kennedy is naturally funny. But now that he's being taken seriously, he's trying to become an anodyne mainstream politician. Politicians in the Labour Party today have become amongst the most passionless, soulless and humour-less bunch of human beings ever. At least Dennis Healy, one of the most rightwing of the Labour old guard, had a personality and some wit. 'New' Labour has become sanitised by being 'new' and by being in government. After leaving the Cabinet, you can see the difference in how Robin Cook now is. He's been personally and politically liberated by resigning. He's started being funny again.

GG: Do you think the far left has been particularly humourless?

MS: It has done but I think the accusation has been exaggerated, and has often come from the right. Of course, all stereotypes have a kernel of truth to them – they have to in order to stand up. Anyone who has been involved with the far left for half an hour will know that the robots do exist. There is the pomposity that you are right and no other view is valid. But I think it's unfair to say that the far left is any more humourless than other political organisations. The right and the middle class liberal left and feminist left can be just as pompous and self-righteous. It's true of any small group or minority view that takes itself seriously in its endeavour to change the world around it. And of course, once you take yourself so seriously, you have the right to be taken the piss out of.

GG: How can humour be used in socialist politics to attract a wider audience? For example, can it have the function of opening up a cultural front to the work of the left?

MS: For a start, working class people are more likely, not less likely, to be attracted to a left that can take the piss out of itself. But sometimes, this kind of thing can happen organically. Some of the most inspiring things I've been to have been benefit gigs and some of the most appalling things I've been to have been benefit gigs. In Europe, there is a much wider and more vibrant tradition of mixing politics and culture on the left, especially where the Communist parties have been significant players. The only thing that we have had in this country that was similar were the Anti-Nazi League carnivals like Rock Against Racism in the 1970s.

GG: What made you write *Reasons to be Cheerful?*

MS: I just thought that having been on the far left for

over twenty years would make an interesting read for a number of reasons for those who either have or haven't been on the far left. One is about playing a small part in the making of history from the miners' strike and the poll tax to the fall of Thatcher. Another is that as a comic, I have an outsider mentality with which to look at the far left even though I've been part of the far left. Therefore, when you get a march of ten people and six of the people are in one group and don't want the other four to be there because they're in a different group, I can think: 'You're all fucking nuts!' Of course, if readers took from it that the whole of the left is fucking nuts, then that would be a pity because that's not what I believe.

GG: Would you agree that humour and wit are every-where in everyday life but are not necessarily recog-nised as such? And following from this, that if their humour is about people's own lives and the lives of others it has a political content and is a political man-ifestation?

MS: Definitely. Today, people use the internet and e-mail for this at the office and in the home so that if something happens in one place it can start going round the world half an hour later. Of course, some-times the political meaning of the humour is dreadful, sometimes it's not. I got dropped home the other night by a Ghanaian taxi driver. We were chatting about the war in Iraq and he said it was like someone who comes around and takes away the father that you despise and gives you a new one and expects you to be happy. He said the point is it wasn't the role of someone else to do that for you. So you could see how that could be funny or even worked up into a comic routine against the Americans. In comedy, as in many other things in life, if you look like you don't mean it, then you look like a twat. So sincerity is important to comedy and even more to comedy with a political edge.

Chapter 3

Round-table Discussion with Colin Fox, Rosie Kane and Carolyn Leckie

Introduction

All three MSPs have west of Scotland backgrounds and this seems to be the general basis for, and context of, the combination and fusion of their humour and politics. It is part of their personae. It is part of who they are and where they have come from. Their humour is used in a considered way to make points more sharply and more incisively than a more serious and longer political response could. It is particularly used to respond to criticism and to allow them to get through tedious and boring experiences such as meetings inside and outside Parliament. But there are also differences between the three in the way they use their humour. Carolyn's is darker, angrier and more biting and cutting, which she attributes to her unconsciously developed personal coping and survival strategy during her teenage years as well as her Protestant background. By contrast, Rosie with an Irish and Catholic background, speaks and thinks in a way that is peppered with wit and humour in the manner of both considered remarks and flow of consciousness. She says she 'thinks in pictures', no doubt where colour and light and shade are important.

Again, by contrast, Colin has a consistent eye for what is funny and humour *per se*. It seems that, for Colin, life and politics are but a constant source of material for observing the lighter side of dark things and the darker side of light things. This round-table discussion interview was conducted in October 2004.

Round-table Discussion

Gregor Gall (GG): Would you say that your use of humour is inherently part of you: it's not something you are consciously trying to do?

Carolyn Leckie (CL): It depends on the environment actually but it's really a sub-conscious thing on my part.

Rosie Kane (RK): It's just the way I react to things. Sometimes I use it because the atmosphere of a meeting is really heavy, but sometimes I use it just to cut to the chase. Instead of reading a whole page of something, a joke can just get to the point in an instant. When you're speaking at a meeting you get a sense of how to tell a story in order to reel people in, get them interested in what you're saying and how to carry them along with you.

GG: So your humour predates becoming active in politics? Were you humorous when you were kids?

RK: I was.

GG: Was this a coping mechanism against boredom

and bullying? Was it about wanting to stand out and be liked?

RK: I became the school shed entertainer.

CL: For me it was an antidote to being seen to be clever and a swot, which weren't good things to be seen to be in the Gorbals. It was a way of rebelling and a way of protecting myself.

Colin Fox (CF): When people used to ask me what I wanted to be when I left school, I used to say a priest or a comedian. For me, it's the classic thing about comedy: using humour can be defensive, it can be about wanting to be loved and be secure, and it's about not wanting to deal with the heavy stuff all the time.

CL: There are differences between how the three of us use humour. I'm more sarcastic and I use it more as a weapon, whether it's defensive or offensive. I hope that it's always aimed against the class enemy.

RK: Carolyn has a poisoned tickle stick!

CF: I find it hard to use humour on people I don't know.

GG: Do you think about the humour you're going to use before you use it or does it come out like a stream of consciousness?

CL: Sometimes it's like a stream of consciousness. I don't plan to be funny or sarcastic, it's off the cuff. But in the chamber or elsewhere it's premeditated because you don't get the chance to say it right away. The creation of it is spontaneous but sometimes you need to store it up for later use.

CF: I find that when I write a speech and I put something funny in it, it usually falls flat. The reason why spontaneity is usually better and works is because there's energy, tension and passion to it that you don't get with something that's contrived. Carolyn's humour seems to be generated out of the electricity of the situation at the time.

GG: Presumably you are either sufficiently confident about using humour the way you do or you just don't care what people think of you?

CL: You're not looking for the approval of politicians and the other political parties.

RK: You're also trying to avoid their manner and their language, and saying 'I'm not doing it the way you do it'. But sometimes, because you could be too brutal or it could be misconstrued in the media, you do self-censor yourself.

GG: When you speak publicly, do you consciously speak as you would do in a private conversation, in the vernacular?

CL: I think we speak as normally in public as we do in private. It's about trying to hang on to our identity, of who we are, and about sending a message to the establishment that we're not conforming. We don't want to patronise or insult ordinary people by talking differently because we're MSPs. But we're aware of how other people in Parliament want to paint us as stupid, as scheme-ies, so we do balance it a little.

CF: I just try to be myself. I can't be anything else.

GG: Why is humour useful in politics? Is it useful to use humour to be able to relate to people?

RK: When I've come away from a public meeting the things I remember are the things that made me smile and laugh, and I can connect these things with the wider issues. I don't want to come away with a headache. Otherwise, meetings can be too intensive. They have to be accessible.

CF: Coming from a Trotskyist background, I think I stored up my humour for decades because you weren't allowed to be funny. It was all dead serious. I remember in the early 1990s when the Militant was making 200 redundancies of full-time staff, we had a big meeting about it and the atmosphere was so terrible and po-faced. I had to cut through that so I went round the building putting up posters using the lefty slogans: 'They say cut back, we say fightback!' and 'Open the books!' They were taken down. At the meeting, Peter Taaffe, the leader of Militant, went ballistic, saying how dare someone try to introduce some levity into this situation. I never let on at the beginning of the meeting that it was me. As the meeting wore on and everyone was knackered, having started at 9am and now being nearly 5pm, when it came to my turn to speak, I got up and said, 'Can I have my posters back?' If I'd said that at the beginning of the meeting, I would have been added to the list of redundancies.

GG: Is there anyone else in the Parliament that is funny?

RK: Occasionally Alex Neil.

CL: Occasionally Phil Gallie.

CF: Occasionally Margo MacDonald. But there's so few of them. If you remember Dennis Skinner, there's a balance to be struck so that you don't end up as being seen as an idiot.

GG: Would you agree that a lot of politicians become sanitised so that they become incapable of being humorous?

CL: I think that politicians' ability to communicate is related to their politics. So it's entirely predictable that Labour MSPs are safe. They haven't got the independence of mind or spirit so they can't be funny. People who suck up other people's arses can't be funny.

CF: You've got to have passion if you're going to be funny.

RK: Labour MSPs will no more cry than tell a joke so that's the other side of it. They will not exhibit emotion. They don't want to be outside the machine.

GG: What about Tommy Sheridan?

CL: His humour is more staged. I think he stays awake

at night thinking up jokes and writing them down. He's a different personality.

CF: He doesn't see humour as an effective way of operating.

CL: The left has traditionally been hierarchical, where the leadership provides all the answers. It's quite pessimistic about people's ability to learn and develop. Humour helps cut across that.

RK: But humour is also honest because it's impulsive and it's an instant reaction to things.

Chapter 4
Colin Fox, SSP List MSP for the Lothians

Colin has become known by friends and foes as the Red Fox, the Fox Trot, the Sly Fox, the MSP for Karaoke West, variously deemed to be leader of the Singing Socialist Party and the Silly Stunts Party. But revered for his wise cracks, quick wit and quotable quotes, Colin burst onto the 'world stage' of mainstream politics with two memorable actions.

The first was demonstrating his athletic prowess on the night of being elected at the Edinburgh Meadowbank count in May 2003. He jumped over barriers and punched the air in a burst of unashamed and untamed joy, only to be stopped by running out of space and out of the building (via the fire exit). The second, a month later, was bringing disruption to the swearing in ceremony at the opening of the second session of the Scottish Parliament by singing Robert Burns' 'A Man's A Man For A' That' as an alternative to taking the oath of allegiance to the Queen. On reflection, he said instead of singing two and a half verses before being stopped by the Presiding Officer, he should have stuck to just one verse, as advised by SSP leader, Tommy Sheridan MSP. The *Scotsman Guide to Scottish Politics* commented: 'In truth, he can neither dance nor sing outstandingly well but both occasions were unforgettable nonetheless'.

He has been a sporadic and guerrilla-like columnist in the *Edinburgh Evening News, Scottish Mirror, Morning Star, Mirror, Scotland on Sunday,* and the *Scottish Socialist Voice.* He is also author of the best-selling *Motherwell is won for Moscow: The Story of Walter Newbold – Britain's first Communist MP and Lenin's Man in Motherwell,* published by Scottish Militant Labour in 1992. (Bulk purchases are still available at discounted prices from Colin. Hurry while stocks last!)

Colin re-founded the Edinburgh People's Festival in 2002 as a necessary corrective to the commercialisation and social exclusion of the existing Festivals and played a leading role in relaunching the annual May Day Demonstration in Edinburgh in 2001. At the launch of Leftfield at the Edinburgh Festival in 2004, Colin performed a turn in the 'Socialist Stars In Their Eyes' event by singing as Matt McGinn and Hamish Imlach.

He is also a part-time, non-profit making entrepreneur: with the help of some friends with computing skills, he has produced a series of politically humorous posters. One example, to the form, design and colour of the Sex Pistol's first album cover, states: 'Never mind the Blairites, here's the Scottish Socialist Party'. Another, with the pictorial background of a scene from *The Simpsons* and photographs of the then four main party leaders in Scotland (Jack McConnell, John Swinney, David McLetchie and Jim Wallace) resting on clouds, has an absent Homer saying: 'D'oh, they're all in Mr

Burns' pocket!' A third has the eye of Channel 4's *Big Brother* series, with the words 'To evict Tony, call …'.

His other claims to notoriety are that he is the only male Parliamentarian with an earring and a haircut described as a 'hedgehog in a gale'. One of my earliest memories is of Colin turning up from Edinburgh to direct SSP campaign operations in the Falkirk by-election in 2000. He gave some orders to campaigners and then promptly went off to get his hair cut before returning to give more orders.

After a year in Parliament, the view of the former *Scotsman* Parliamentary Sketch Writer, Robert McNeil, of the Red Fox went as follows:

> *Nice young man, but brings a defeated air to the chamber. … [His] buccaneering approach [offered to] lighten up the place. However … the place has beaten him. He doesn't believe he's going to change anyone's mind and so doesn't see the point. But that isn't the point. Needs to decide whether he really wants to make a go of Parliament, in which case he could be good. (3/5) (Scotsman 3 May 2004)*

Of course, that depends on whether you see Parliament as an end in itself or as a platform with which to address people outside Parliament.

The assessment of the *Scottish Socialist Voice* (9 July 2004) of Colin's first year was rather different:

> *School closures are a major issue in the Lothians and Colin has been campaigning hard with the parents of a number of schools threatened with closure. As*

organiser of the Edinburgh May Day, Colin spoke alongside Arthur Scargill to mark the 20th anniversary of the Miners' Strike. As chair of the Edinburgh People's Festival, Colin was again instrumental in bringing 'the world's greatest arts celebration' to the city communities normally excluded from the 'official', highly commercialised version.

Political Inspiration

Like many of his generation, he found inspiration in the radical theatre group 7:84 and its seminal work 'The Cheviot, the Stag and the Black, Black Oil.' He also cites the emergence of 'political punk rock' as a catalyst for his thinking in the early 1980s. The ascendancy of Tony Benn in the same period, who ran for Deputy Leader of the Labour Party in 1981 and almost won, was a landmark in his early years and led him to join the Labour Party Young Socialists (LPYS) in unemployment ravaged Motherwell at that time.

Leisure and Pastime Interests

Sport - he jogs, reads non-fiction and travels.

Biography

Born 1959 in Motherwell and brother of Carol Fox, Labour candidate in Edinburgh West in the 1999 and 2003 Scottish Parliament elections. Joined the Labour Party in 1978 after seeing the difference in salaries between the directors and secretaries when auditing company accounts. Joined Militant in 1981. Worked as Militant organiser in Lanarkshire and London between 1983-1995. Returned from London in 1995 to help found the Scottish Socialist Alliance in 1996 and worked as the SSA and then SSP Lothians Regional Organiser from 1996 to 2003. Stood unsuccessfully in the 1999 Scottish Parliament elections as the lead list SSP candidate. Also contested the 2001 Westminster Parliamentary election. Lives in Edinburgh with partner, Zillah, a midwife, and two children, Laura, aged 9 and Ciaran, aged 4.

The Revolutionary Witticisms of Colin Fox

Coming Back from Down Under Without a Suntan

> In our party coming back from anywhere with a tan would be interpreted as a leadership challenge.

On His New Job as MSP

> MSPs don't work Mondays and Fridays, so it's a really long weekend. Four months' holidays, £48,000 a year and a three-day week. Man, this is socialism!

(Like all SSP MSPs, Colin donates half his MSP's salary to the SSP)

Having an Epiphany

> I've just found the parliamentary road to socialism. It

was right next to the weapons of mass destruction in Iraq.

On That Singing

Laura told her classmates the next day that her dad had been chucked out of the Parliament because 'his singing was that bad'.

On New Labour's New NHS

I thought kidology was the children's ward at the new Edinburgh Royal Infirmary until I discovered PFI.

Reply to the Master of the Royal Household, Declining an Invitation to the 2003 Garden Party to Meet the Queen at Holyrood Palace

Aff with her heid!

Responding to Another Royal Invitation to Meet His Royal Highness the Prince of Wales in 2004

Nice to know his mum doesn't hold a grudge. Aff with his ears!

Off With His Heid: No Job Too Small (à la Advert in Shop Window)

Being Politically Honest and Declaring Class War on the Edinbourgeoisie

(SSP members handed out £1m of fake £20 notes in Edinburgh to highlight how much ordinary people would save under the party's proposed Scottish Service Tax):

> It was a blatant attempt to buy votes on May 1. It's a fair cop. All the other parties deny they are trying to buy votes but we have decided to come clean. ... Of course, we intend to get our million back by taxing the rich at a higher rate. So look out up there at Jenners and Harvey Nicks, here we come!

Acting Aspirations

(Responding to Tommy Sheridan being compared to George Clooney):

> I see myself as Charles Bronson. He went on to do *Death Wish* and I'll gladly supply that for the Tories.

On Political Opponents' Lack of Scientific Rigour

(Reacting to an opinion poll showing continued high SSP support):

> When this figure was produced last month our opponents immediately rubbished it. But this confirms this is not a blip. It is a trend. To rubbish one set of figures is unfortunate, but to rubbish two sets is carelessness.

(Visiting Floors Castle at Kelso, the ancient seat of the Duke of Roxburgh, a couple of years ago, Colin noticed the visitors' book was placed strategically beside an intimate photo of the Duke, his wife and their two children at the wedding reception for Charles and Diana inside Buckingham Palace. So in the column for 'Comments', Colin wrote):

Down wi' the monarchy. Aff wi' their heids. Executions our speciality, no job considered too small. Call the SSP on 0131 557 0426 and ask for Colin.

Recounting Debating Student Militancy with Disgraced Former Tory Minister Jonathan Aitken at the Oxford Union.

> Instead of giving the students a quote from Lenin because I figured they'd never heard of him, I decided to give them a quote from Oprah Winfrey. She said: 'If you don't stand for something, you'll fall for anything'.

After His Lap of Joyous Honour at Meadowbank

> I was like a kangaroo on speed.

After Seeing His Lap of Honour on Television

> Of course, it was finely choreographed in advance.

(Colin's athletic prowess became the subject of a question on *University Challenge* in 2004.)

Explaining his Qualifications to Sit on the Scottish Parliament's Justice 2 Committee

[Of the SSP MSPs]: I think it's because I am the only one who hasn't been to the jail.

Borrowing Money off Sean Connery for Electioneering in 2003

We support independence too. It appears Sir Sean doesn't know that. I reminded him that we are for an independent socialist Scotland where the rich pay their fair share in taxes. I hope he'll be generous. After all, we're skint. It costs £5,000 to stand Holyrood candidates across the Lothians. ... (Upon being told that if the SSP didn't have the cash, they could put up a bond) ... Bond? Well, I just might know who to speak too ...

(Sir Sean Connery is well known as a supporter of the SNP and Scottish independence.)

Trying to Win over Sir Sean, Part 2

(Colin wrote out four huge placards bearing the following notice and joined in an assembled 'invited SNP guests and party members' to greet Alex Salmond and Sir Sean Connery as they arrived for an SNP morale-raising rally at Edinburgh's EICC conference centre in 1999):

Vote Schottish Shochialisht Party!

(Sir Sean was often dubbed the SNP MP for Marbella West.)

On Giving a Helping Hand to David Sneddon, Winner of Fame Academy in 2002

It [the Edinburgh People's Festival] was one of the last gigs he played before he went on to Fame Academy. ... We gave David his first big break. ... I've sent him an e-mail saying we hope he's OK for next year. We're awaiting a reply to say he'll fit us in between the London Palladium and the SECC.

On the Reception at Holyrood from Other MSPs

I felt about as welcome as a hedgehog on South Uist.

(Hedgehogs have been culled on South Uist for a number of years).

Pleased to Meet You, MSP

(Asked by a constituent what the correct form of address was for a Member of the Scottish Parliament, Colin replied):

Your MSPness, of course. ... I am told it is especially popular at Easter Road and Tynecastle when Brian Montieth and David McLetchie attend matches. Although I understand it is abridged there just to 'Pness, Pness'.

(Montieth and McLetchie are leading and well-known Tories. Easter Road and Tynecastle are the home of Edinburgh's premier football teams.)

On Unity and Disunity on the Left at the May Day Demonstration, London 2002

> There were 57 varieties of socialism outside the Marx Memorial Library in Clerkenwell. And all of them calling for a united socialist party. You just had to laugh. ... There were a couple of cross-dressing socialists, bedecked in twinset and pearls, with signs 'Auntie Capitalists'.

Advocating International Working Class Solidarity

(The Turkish Communist Party poster in London proclaimed 'Mao, more than ever'. Colin invited these comrades to the Edinburgh May Day Parade):

> Well, you know what they say – the Mao, the merrier!

Asking for Legal Help to Deal with the Theft of Party Property (Illustrated with Poster)

> I sent Downing Street a courtesy copy of our highly popular poster of Mrs Thatcher turning into Tony Blair some months ago. I suppose that since imitation is, as they say, the sincerest form of flattery, I should be proud they nicked our notion. ... I must confess I do not see this trend – Labour stealing our ideas – continuing. ... But I shall be consulting our lawyers to see how we can protect our intellectual property rights.

No Party Pooper of New Labour

It's not the winning that counts, it's the taking apart of New Labour that matters.

Dealing with the Capitalist Media at SSP Press Conferences

No matter how difficult your questions, we pledge not to punch you in the mouth.

Disagreeing with the Party Leader

How many seats would the SSP win in the 2001 general election?
Tommy Sheridan: 'None.'
Colin Fox: 'All of them.'

Contesting the Falkirk West Westminster Parliament By-Election, December 2000

If you really believe electing another New Labour MP will make one iota of difference then you might as well hang up your stocking and start believing in Santa.

(Voters did elect another New Labour MP, Major Eric Joyce. Merry Christmas, Santa!)

On Access at Last to the Mainstream Media During the Falkirk West By-Election

Can I say how nice it is to be here in the studio with the rest of you'se. Normally, the SSP is reduced to ringing in from a phonebox somewhere outside Carluke.

More from Falkirk

(On the first day of the Falkirk West by-election, the SSP occupied the premises of a local Sheriff Officers, Love and Co, because of their hounding of people for outstanding poll tax debts. Murray Ritchie, the *Herald's* political editor telephoned in, seeking news. He asked Colin what kind of a start the SSP campaign had enjoyed):

Brilliant. Couldn't be better. Our candidate is in the jail.

(SSP candidate Iain Hunter had been arrested and kept in jail overnight for alleged 'breach of the peace' at the offices of the Sheriff Officers. The charges were subsequently dropped.)

On Showing Brotherly Solidarity in the Face of State Oppression in a Tea Shop

Police Officer: Are you Iain Hunter?
Colin: Me, Iain Hunter? Naw, that's him over there.
Iain is duly frog-marched out as Colin and others take their tea.

(Conversation following the occupation of the offices of a sheriff officer.)

Fighting the Firrhill Local Council By-Election in Edinburgh, April 2000

> If you've got a scooby, you won't vote Scobie. It's not the catchiest slogan in the world. But I bet the Labour candidate won't like it.

(Andrew Scobie, the Labour candidate, won and Colin came fourth, ahead of the Liberal Democrats.)

Being Outcast by the Party Leader, 2000

> We are sometimes seen as being a Glasgow-only party. And I have to say that sometimes we are eclipsed by Tommy's superstar status – and his suntan.

Commenting on Scotland's Internal Divisions, 2000

> We aim to make our mark in Edinburgh. Tommy is a big asset but he is a Glasgow MSP and you know what the east/west divide is like. When they took down the Berlin wall, they rebuilt it at Livingston.

Being Aware of Scotland's Internal Divisions and the Benefits of a Marxist Education

> I declare an interest – perhaps it is a confession as I am a Lothians MSP – I am a lifelong Motherwell fan. … It is always a joy to hear Karl Marx mentioned in the chamber. Whereas my colleague Mr Swinburne got it right, the minister – typically – got his quote wrong, so it is back to the drawing board for him. …

In response to Mr McLetchie's remarks, I could not help but recall the words of Lenin—no less—who advised the likes of Mr McLetchie: 'You're better getting a kopeck from 1,000 workers than having the backing of one multi-millionaire'.

(In a parliamentary debate about the perilous financial state of Scottish football.)

On Blood Curdling Enemies

I know that Labour members are anxious. They have the smell of blood in their nostrils and want to get on to punishment, punishment, punishment.

Political Aspirations and Predictions

(Invited to Australia and New Zealand by the Socialist Alliances there):

They are keen to hear of the success of the SSP in Scotland. But we might have something to learn from them, since the New Zealand Alliance has been in coalition government with Labour. So we will get advice on how to drive a hard bargain for 2007, when we have 20 SSP MSPs!

(Could Colin be accused of making fantastic Tommy-like predictions?)

Responding to Critics from Australia, 2003

(SNP MSP Kenny MacAskill accused Colin of gallivanting around the southern hemisphere instead of representing his constituents):

> I immediately e-mailed Mr MacAskill and told him I couldn't give a XXXX for his cheap shots.

When Told by the Australian Broadcasting Corporation Interviewer that the Socialist Alliance was Very Much on the Fringe of Australian Politics

> Well, I'm here to help them grow into a bushy perm.

On Being Asked By a Journalist in Sydney What the Purpose of His Visit Was

> I've come to seek regime change!

(John Howard, Tory premier, was re-elected in 2004.)

More Dispatches from Australia

(Addressing his audience at the Socialist Alliance state conference in Australia):

> Actually, I travelled all this way to seek compensation for that atrocious portrayal of William Wallace by Mel Gibson. I will be standing by the door with a bucket for you to put your donations in.

Speaking at the Edinburgh Tenants' Federation AGM on Opposition to the Council's Stock Transfer Plans

> Million pound houses are ten a penny in Edinburgh.

On the Running Down of Scottish Opera Using Mixed Metaphors

(Pie-man MSP Frank McAveety was the then Minister for Culture):

> This is the act of the cultural philistine in charge of the asylum.

On Brian Wilson MP, the Then Minister at the Department of Trade and Industry, Following His Claim that List MSPs were a 'waste of space'

> If anyone round here is a waste of space round here, it is Brian Wilson. He is so under-employed Tony Blair sent him to Baghdad as a salesman.

The Edinburgh People's Festival, Allegedly Sponsored by Heinekin!

The EPF refreshes the parts of Edinburgh that other festivals don't reach.

The Development of Language is a Dynamic Process

> Scunneration – is that a real word? Anyway, we're going to be scunnered if we don't get more help and more people involved because me and the small numbers responsible for organising this are knackered.

(Colin making an appeal at the debate 'Whose culture is it any way?' in the Edinburgh People's Festival for help to make the EPF bigger.)

The Bite of the Reservoir Dogs

(In 1999, responding to lack of coverage of the SSP during Scottish Elections, Colin and three others stormed a business conference extolling the 'profit opportunities of PFI contracts', dressed as the characters from Tarantino's *Reservoirs Dogs* – Mr Ron Brown, Mr Derrick White among them – saying):

> The heist on the public purse which will inevitably go wrong.

On the Last Day at the Mound Before Going to Holyrood Proper

(Presiding Officer George Reid defended his decision to charge members of the public £3.50 to see round the new £431m Parliament from SSP criticism that the public had paid quite enough and demanding the issue be debated. He challenged MSPs to make Holyrood a success, insisting: 'After all, it's not the buildings which make the Parliament. Colin interrupted with an aimed heckle):

> No, it's the building workers!

On the Dire State on Scotland's National Football Team in 2004 (or any other year)

(The Republic of Ireland proposed a joint bid with Scotland to host the 2012 Euro tournament):

> The prospect of Scotland seeing the best of European

(Visiting Floors Castle at Kelso, the ancient seat of the Duke of Roxburgh, a couple of years ago, Colin noticed the visitors' book was placed strategically beside an intimate photo of the Duke, his wife and their two children at the wedding reception for Charles and Diana inside Buckingham Palace. So in the column for 'Comments', Colin wrote):

Down wi' the monarchy. Aff wi' their heids. Executions our speciality, no job considered too small. Call the SSP on 0131 557 0426 and ask for Colin.

Recounting Debating Student Militancy with Disgraced Former Tory Minister Jonathan Aitken at the Oxford Union.

> Instead of giving the students a quote from Lenin because I figured they'd never heard of him, I decided to give them a quote from Oprah Winfrey. She said: 'If you don't stand for something, you'll fall for anything'.

After His Lap of Joyous Honour at Meadowbank

> I was like a kangaroo on speed.

After Seeing His Lap of Honour on Television

> Of course, it was finely choreographed in advance.

(Colin's athletic prowess became the subject of a question on *University Challenge* in 2004.)

Explaining his Qualifications to Sit on the Scottish Parliament's Justice 2 Committee

[Of the SSP MSPs]: I think it's because I am the only one who hasn't been to the jail.

Borrowing Money off Sean Connery for Electioneering in 2003

We support independence too. It appears Sir Sean doesn't know that. I reminded him that we are for an independent socialist Scotland where the rich pay their fair share in taxes. I hope he'll be generous. After all, we're skint. It costs £5,000 to stand Holyrood candidates across the Lothians. ... (Upon being told that if the SSP didn't have the cash, they could put up a bond) ... Bond? Well, I just might know who to speak too ...

(Sir Sean Connery is well known as a supporter of the SNP and Scottish independence.)

Trying to Win over Sir Sean, Part 2

(Colin wrote out four huge placards bearing the following notice and joined in an assembled 'invited SNP guests and party members' to greet Alex Salmond and Sir Sean Connery as they arrived for an SNP morale-raising rally at Edinburgh's EICC conference centre in 1999):

Vote Schottish Shochialisht Party!

(Sir Sean was often dubbed the SNP MP for Marbella West.)

On Giving a Helping Hand to David Sneddon, Winner of Fame Academy in 2002

> It [the Edinburgh People's Festival] was one of the last gigs he played before he went on to Fame Academy. ... We gave David his first big break. ... I've sent him an e-mail saying we hope he's OK for next year. We're awaiting a reply to say he'll fit us in between the London Palladium and the SECC.

On the Reception at Holyrood from Other MSPs

> I felt about as welcome as a hedgehog on South Uist.

(Hedgehogs have been culled on South Uist for a number of years).

Pleased to Meet You, MSP

(Asked by a constituent what the correct form of address was for a Member of the Scottish Parliament, Colin replied):

> Your MSPness, of course. ... I am told it is especially popular at Easter Road and Tynecastle when Brian Montieth and David McLetchie attend matches. Although I understand it is abridged there just to 'Pness, Pness'.

(Montieth and McLetchie are leading and well-known Tories. Easter Road and Tynecastle are the home of Edinburgh's premier football teams.)

Being Politically Honest and Declaring Class War on the Edinbourgeoisie

(SSP members handed out £1m of fake £20 notes in Edinburgh to highlight how much ordinary people would save under the party's proposed Scottish Service Tax):

> It was a blatant attempt to buy votes on May 1. It's a fair cop. All the other parties deny they are trying to buy votes but we have decided to come clean. ... Of course, we intend to get our million back by taxing the rich at a higher rate. So look out up there at Jenners and Harvey Nicks, here we come!

Acting Aspirations

(Responding to Tommy Sheridan being compared to George Clooney):

> I see myself as Charles Bronson. He went on to do *Death Wish* and I'll gladly supply that for the Tories.

On Political Opponents' Lack of Scientific Rigour

(Reacting to an opinion poll showing continued high SSP support):

> When this figure was produced last month our opponents immediately rubbished it. But this confirms this is not a blip. It is a trend. To rubbish one set of figures is unfortunate, but to rubbish two sets is carelessness.

On Unity and Disunity on the Left at the May Day Demonstration, London 2002

> There were 57 varieties of socialism outside the Marx Memorial Library in Clerkenwell. And all of them calling for a united socialist party. You just had to laugh. ... There were a couple of cross-dressing socialists, bedecked in twinset and pearls, with signs 'Auntie Capitalists'.

Advocating International Working Class Solidarity

(The Turkish Communist Party poster in London proclaimed 'Mao, more than ever'. Colin invited these comrades to the Edinburgh May Day Parade):

> Well, you know what they say – the Mao, the merrier!

Asking for Legal Help to Deal with the Theft of Party Property (Illustrated with Poster)

> I sent Downing Street a courtesy copy of our highly popular poster of Mrs Thatcher turning into Tony Blair some months ago. I suppose that since imitation is, as they say, the sincerest form of flattery, I should be proud they nicked our notion. ... I must confess I do not see this trend – Labour stealing our ideas – continuing. ... But I shall be consulting our lawyers to see how we can protect our intellectual property rights.

No Party Pooper of New Labour

It's not the winning that counts, it's the taking apart of New Labour that matters.

Dealing with the Capitalist Media at SSP Press Conferences

No matter how difficult your questions, we pledge not to punch you in the mouth.

Disagreeing with the Party Leader

How many seats would the SSP win in the 2001 general election?
Tommy Sheridan: 'None.'
Colin Fox: 'All of them.'

Contesting the Falkirk West Westminster Parliament By-Election, December 2000

If you really believe electing another New Labour MP will make one iota of difference then you might as well hang up your stocking and start believing in Santa.

(Voters did elect another New Labour MP, Major Eric Joyce. Merry Christmas, Santa!)

On Access at Last to the Mainstream Media During the Falkirk West By-Election

Can I say how nice it is to be here in the studio with the rest of you'se. Normally, the SSP is reduced to ringing in from a phonebox somewhere outside Carluke.

More from Falkirk

(On the first day of the Falkirk West by-election, the SSP occupied the premises of a local Sheriff Officers, Love and Co, because of their hounding of people for outstanding poll tax debts. Murray Ritchie, the *Herald's* political editor telephoned in, seeking news. He asked Colin what kind of a start the SSP campaign had enjoyed):

Brilliant. Couldn't be better. Our candidate is in the jail.

(SSP candidate Iain Hunter had been arrested and kept in jail overnight for alleged 'breach of the peace' at the offices of the Sheriff Officers. The charges were subsequently dropped.)

On Showing Brotherly Solidarity in the Face of State Oppression in a Tea Shop

Police Officer: Are you Iain Hunter?
Colin: Me, Iain Hunter? Naw, that's him over there.
Iain is duly frog-marched out as Colin and others take their tea.

(Conversation following the occupation of the offices of a sheriff officer.)

Fighting the Firrhill Local Council By-Election in Edinburgh, April 2000

> If you've got a scooby, you won't vote Scobie. It's not the catchiest slogan in the world. But I bet the Labour candidate won't like it.

(Andrew Scobie, the Labour candidate, won and Colin came fourth, ahead of the Liberal Democrats.)

Being Outcast by the Party Leader, 2000

> We are sometimes seen as being a Glasgow-only party. And I have to say that sometimes we are eclipsed by Tommy's superstar status – and his suntan.

Commenting on Scotland's Internal Divisions, 2000

> We aim to make our mark in Edinburgh. Tommy is a big asset but he is a Glasgow MSP and you know what the east/west divide is like. When they took down the Berlin wall, they rebuilt it at Livingston.

Being Aware of Scotland's Internal Divisions and the Benefits of a Marxist Education

> I declare an interest – perhaps it is a confession as I am a Lothians MSP – I am a lifelong Motherwell fan. … It is always a joy to hear Karl Marx mentioned in the chamber. Whereas my colleague Mr Swinburne got it right, the minister – typically – got his quote wrong, so it is back to the drawing board for him. …

In response to Mr McLetchie's remarks, I could not help but recall the words of Lenin—no less—who advised the likes of Mr McLetchie: 'You're better getting a kopeck from 1,000 workers than having the backing of one multi-millionaire'.

(In a parliamentary debate about the perilous financial state of Scottish football.)

On Blood Curdling Enemies

I know that Labour members are anxious. They have the smell of blood in their nostrils and want to get on to punishment, punishment, punishment.

Political Aspirations and Predictions

(Invited to Australia and New Zealand by the Socialist Alliances there):

They are keen to hear of the success of the SSP in Scotland. But we might have something to learn from them, since the New Zealand Alliance has been in coalition government with Labour. So we will get advice on how to drive a hard bargain for 2007, when we have 20 SSP MSPs!

(Could Colin be accused of making fantastic Tommy-like predictions?)

Responding to Critics from Australia, 2003

(SNP MSP Kenny MacAskill accused Colin of gallivant-

ing around the southern hemisphere instead of representing his constituents):

> I immediately e-mailed Mr MacAskill and told him I
> couldn't give a XXXX for his cheap shots.

When Told by the Australian Broadcasting Corporation
Interviewer that the Socialist Alliance was Very Much on
the Fringe of Australian Politics

> Well, I'm here to help them grow into a bushy perm.

On Being Asked By a Journalist in Sydney What the
Purpose of His Visit Was

> I've come to seek regime change!

(John Howard, Tory premier, was re-elected in 2004.)

More Dispatches from Australia

(Addressing his audience at the Socialist Alliance state
conference in Australia):

> Actually, I travelled all this way to seek compensation
> for that atrocious portrayal of William Wallace by Mel
> Gibson. I will be standing by the door with a bucket
> for you to put your donations in.

Speaking at the Edinburgh Tenants' Federation AGM on
Opposition to the Council's Stock Transfer Plans

> Million pound houses are ten a penny in Edinburgh.

On the Running Down of Scottish Opera Using Mixed Metaphors

(Pie-man MSP Frank McAveety was the then Minister for Culture):

> This is the act of the cultural philistine in charge of the asylum.

On Brian Wilson MP, the Then Minister at the Department of Trade and Industry, Following His Claim that List MSPs were a 'waste of space'

> If anyone round here is a waste of space round here, it is Brian Wilson. He is so under-employed Tony Blair sent him to Baghdad as a salesman.

The Edinburgh People's Festival, Allegedly Sponsored by Heinekin!

The EPF refreshes the parts of Edinburgh that other festivals don't reach.

The Development of Language is a Dynamic Process

> Scunneration – is that a real word? Anyway, we're going to be scunnered if we don't get more help and more people involved because me and the small numbers responsible for organising this are knackered.

(Colin making an appeal at the debate 'Whose culture is it any way?' in the Edinburgh People's Festival for help to make the EPF bigger.)

The Bite of the Reservoir Dogs

(In 1999, responding to lack of coverage of the SSP during Scottish Elections, Colin and three others stormed a business conference extolling the 'profit opportunities of PFI contracts', dressed as the characters from Tarantino's *Reservoirs Dogs* – Mr Ron Brown, Mr Derrick White among them – saying):

The heist on the public purse which will inevitably go wrong.

On the Last Day at the Mound Before Going to Holyrood Proper

(Presiding Officer George Reid defended his decision to charge members of the public £3.50 to see round the new £431m Parliament from SSP criticism that the public had paid quite enough and demanding the issue be debated. He challenged MSPs to make Holyrood a success, insisting: 'After all, it's not the buildings which make the Parliament. Colin interrupted with an aimed heckle):

No, it's the building workers!

On the Dire State on Scotland's National Football Team in 2004 (or any other year)

(The Republic of Ireland proposed a joint bid with Scotland to host the 2012 Euro tournament):

The prospect of Scotland seeing the best of European

football would be a good thing. Besides, the way things are going, the only way Scotland will ever get to the European championships is if they host them.

On the Internationale: Can Young People Understand the Socialist Anthem?

I never really worked out what a starveling is. Every time I hear it I think of skinny birds flying around.

Analysing the American Ruling Class and its Political Representatives

George Bush is like Mr Whippy – you know his name is on the van but he's not the one making the ice cream.

On the New Bear Pit in the New Parliament Building

(Asked of Campbell Martin MSP, as Nicola Sturgeon made her debut as SNP leader at Holyrood facing Jack McConnell at First Minister's Questions):

Is this where you see the dwarfs fighting?

On the First Minister's Ideological Journey: How Best Practice Can Change over Time

What works? Jack McConnell used to believe in managerial socialism. Now, it's just managerialism.

On Deputy First Minister and Lib Dem leader, Jim Wallace.

Who? I much prefer his brother, Gromit.

Why Does the Opposition Have all the Best Actors?

(On hearing that SSP sympathiser and actor, Dougray Scott, is being considered for the role as the new James Bond):

Let them have the old one. We'd sooner have the new one any day.

Orange Coloured Tiny Trots are on the Way: Beware!

(When one colleague suggested that Tommy Sheridan's new baby, to be called Tommy if it's a boy, would probably come out looking like its dad, Colin opined):

That's a rather jaundiced view.

All That Glitters is Not Gold (Part 1)

(His constant refrain on encountering over many weeks each new facet of the new £431 million Parliament building):

I like it. What is it?

All That Glitters is Not Gold (Part 2)

(When asked what he thought of the new £431 million Parliament building):

It's great for £40 million.

(£40 million was the original estimate.)

If A Week is a Long Time in Politics …

(When told that NHS prescription charges were originally introduced in the 1950s to pay for Britain's involvement in the Korean War):

You'd think we'd have paid for it by now!

A Cultural Ambassador in His Spare Time

(Colin told the crowds assembled on Calton Hill in October 2004 to celebrate the opening of the new Parliament building by declaring for a Scottish Republic, that he liked to interrupt tourists he hears on the Royal Mile claiming this or that Queen built this or that city landmark):

She never laid a brick!

You Always Hurt the Ones You Love

(Noticing that the invitation from the Queen was for him and '… Mrs Fox' and since he and Zillah aren't married, that maybe his mum was expecting to go along and accompany him):

Sorry, Mum. I'm a socialist, a republican and a revolutionary.

Chapter 5
Carolyn Leckie, SSP List MSP for Central Scotland

Carolyn was widely known of before being elected to Parliament as a result of her trade union activities. She won Unison's award in 2002 for the best branch recruitment but less acclaim from her national union leadership for leading two successful strikes against low pay by medical secretaries in 2001 and hospital workers in 2002. This provided the media with the material to fit her into its stereotype of the wild-eyed union militant and left-wing agitator. She gained further infamy following the opening of the second session of Parliament in 2003, and from being the first MSP to be suspended from Parliament in 2004 during an attempt to get the case of the striking nursery nurses heard.

According to media commentators, she has a reputation for being simultaneously feisty and a flamboyant dresser, shabbily glamorous and quick-witted with a voice that could strip paint. The outgoing Presiding Officer of the Parliament, Sir David Steel, when he thought his microphone was turned off, commented in a manner befitting the male domination of the chamber and when referring to Carolyn and Rosie that 'the view is certainly going to improve in this Parliament'.

Variously   dubbed   the   Bolshevik   Bruennhilde,

Bolshevik Belle, Bolshevik Boadicea, Scruffy Spice, Trailer Park Trash, MSP for Plunging Necklines and looking like she was 'permanently on a night out', you might be mistaken for thinking that the media strenuously objected to a confident, outspoken, radical woman by referring to what she looks like, rather than to what she says, as a means of political denigration. She has been an occasional columnist in the *Scottish Mirror*, *Scottish Socialist Voice* and *RMT News*.

After a year in Parliament, the view of the former *Scotsman* Parliamentary Sketch Writer, Robert McNeil, of Carolyn was as follows:

> *Carolyn was made for the picketline, not the Parliament. Her lips were made to kiss megaphones. She does get passionate in the chamber, but always acts as if she is in the camp of the enemy. Therefore, she never feels at ease or happy. (3/5)* (*Scotsman* 3 May 2004)

Maybe she will now that she's broken her duck by being the first suspended MSP, when seeking to bring workers' concerns into the chamber.

The assessment of the *Scottish Socialist Voice* (9 July 2004) of Carolyn's first year was rather different:

> *Carolyn has been extremely active in her constituency on a wide range of issues including protests against the Greengairs landfill near Airdrie and the Dunbeth Park PPP scheme, and support for the campaign for a skatepark for young people in Wishaw. Carolyn continues to be a member of UNISON and to play an*

active role in trade union issues, particularly in relation to health.

Her high profile continued: when supporting a Scottish Women Against Pornography protest against the Bank of Scotland, the *Scotsman* diarist commented on the irony that all the politically incorrect snappers wanted photographs of Carolyn to illustrate the action.

Political Inspiration

Carolyn attributes her political awakening to being brought up in an Orange and Masonic household in the Gorbals and beginning to notice poverty, deprivation and injustice around her which did not sit easily with the views predominant in the household, and her father also being a shop steward. This awakening was also informed by her grandfather being a participant in Red Clydeside of the First World War and shortly thereafter, as well as by reading the sections of the Bible dealing with social justice. These came together for her in becoming a socialist.

Leisure and Pastime Interests

Reads novels and biographies, cinema, ballet, classical music, television soap operas, competitive sports and hill walking.

Biography

Born 1965, Glasgow. Administrator with Strathclyde Regional Council 1982-1986 and 1987-1989, where she was a NALGO shop steward. Retrained to become a midwife and practised midwifery between 1995-2003, where she became the Unison branch secretary for the north Glasgow hospitals branch. Led two successful strikes. Joined the SSP in 1998 following involvement in campaigning to stop the closure of Rutherglen maternity unit, where she worked, and contested the 1999 Scottish Parliamentary and 2001 Westminster Parliamentary elections. Carolyn lives in East Kilbride with her two daughters, Lynsey, 18, and Ailidh, 15.

The Revolutionary Witticisms of Carolyn Leckie

The Real Reason Carolyn Couldn't Take the Oath to the Queen

(Following stating 'I believe in an independent socialist republic and I take this oath under very strong protest to a woman who has inherited privilege'):

> Apart from anything else, I don't even know the woman!

Responding to the Accusation that the SSP's 2003 Election Manifesto was Uncosted

> This isn't Countdown and I'm not Carole Vorderman.

On the Link Between Privatisation and National Security

(In response to Labour MSP John Home Robertson arguing that to withdraw the troops now would allow Saddam Hussein back into power):

How, have Reliance got a hold of him?

(SSP policy is to withdraw British troops from Iraq immediately and to end the contract of serial incompetents Reliance Security, private providers of court escort services.)

On Knowing the Price of Everything and the Value of Nothing?

(In response to SNP MSP Stewart Stevenson valuing himself at 48 guineas, the cost of being delivered before the arrival of the free at the point of demand NHS):

Did your maw get a rebate? Did you get a rebate? You should have.

On Not Having Had an Education in the Militant Tendency

(Responding to serial baiter SNP MSP Stewart Stevenson in the manner of *Chewing the Fat*):

Gonnae explain what a Trot is because I dinnae know what it is.

(Similar to Rosie, Carolyn was not a member of Militant, leading both of them to subscribe to the view that they were 'without a box of tricks' that Militant had given its former members like Colin Fox, Frances Curran and Tommy Sheridan in terms of Marxist education.)

On Taxing the Mega-Rich and Another Reason for Scottish Independence

(Following a debate on motorists' speeding ticket fines being index-linked to income):

If we had such a system in Scotland, we'd have made a fortune out of Princess Anne.

(Princess Anne is well-known as a serial law breaker.)

On Personality Cults and Lustful Thoughts

(Commenting simultaneously about the charismatic leadership of Tommy Sheridan and the iconic image of Che Guevara):

We can legislate against idolatry but not against hormones.

Worldly Thoughts on Worthy Culture

Growing up in the Gorbals, Shakespeare seemed about as relevant to me as quantum physics.

Dealing With a One-Man-Band With an Understatement?

If Tommy falls under a bus tomorrow, we'd have a wee wake. It would be a blow, of course.

Analysing the Outcome of the Glasgow Hospital Workers' Strike, 2002

> The minnow piranhas have taken a bite out of a giant multi-national corporation and won.

Nothing to Say? 'As If', Some Might Say!

(On condemning the plight of asylum seekers in Scotland):

> I'm speechless … because I cannot come to terms with the barbarity and depravity of it all. …

The Class Struggle Continues from the Picketline to the Parliament

> In some ways life as an MSP isn't much different from what it was when I was a Unison branch secretary. The battles are the same, the enemy is the same, just the arena is different!

My Intervention is Better than Yours!

> Carolyn: Will the member take an intervention?
> Liberal Democrat MSP Mike Rumbles: No—I have just taken one.
> Carolyn: My intervention is different.

(Asking for an intervention is the parliamentary etiquette for asking if one MSP may interrupt another in order to ask a question or make a point.)

Be Nice and Get Noticed Through Your Interventions!

> Carolyn: Will the minister take an intervention?
>
> Labour MSP Tom McCabe: Sure.
>
> Carolyn: Thank you very much – that was a wee surprise.

Dealing with Political Opponents: 1984 turns into 2004

> Stewart Stevenson is a laugh. I was not going to tell him this, but I will. Last night, my daughter told me that her English class was having the usual end-of-term Christmas debates and that she moved – completely of her own accord – that Stewart Stevenson be placed in Room 101. The class voted unanimously that he should be placed in Room 101. That is about all that I will say.

(SNP MSP Stewart Stevenson has become a 'loony left' and 'red'-baiter of the SSP MSPs.)

Dealing With Political Opponents: Stage Play or Just Unparliamentary Language?

> Carolyn: I beg your pardon. On a point of order, Presiding Officer. Is it not against rule 7.3 of the standing orders for a member to call another member ridiculous?
>
> Deputy Presiding Officer: That is normal debating. Please carry on. [Interruption.] Order, please.
>
> Carolyn: All right. If that is normal debating phraseology—
>
> Liberal Democrat MSP Mike Rumbles: She used it.

Carolyn: I was quoting Mike Rumbles. In the words of my daughter, 'You're a tube.' [Laughter.]

(Background information in parentheses from the official record of the debates in the chamber.)

Like Being Back at School

I was not going to ask to speak but I did not want to be left out. This is the best laugh I have had in here since I started. ... Finally, if he is offering tea for everybody ....

(Carolyn speaking in a debate on the provision of water supply against the position of the Scottish Executive.)

Being the Teacher, Not the Pupil

Will members let me finish? Certain members in the chamber have complained about bad behaviour and rude manners, but I have never met such a bunch of rude and badly behaved people in all my life.

(Carloyn plays to the brunnhilde stereotype beloved of the male political hacks.)

Criticising Those Who Are Not Spontaneous: Have Spin, Try to Travel

(After Labour MSP Hugh Henry's speech):

I have had the privilege of writing my summing-up speech while I have been listening to the debate, which is what I had thought everybody did—but apparently not, because the Executive's summing-up speech is already written and I have a copy of it here.

On the Selling of Public Assets to a Private Concern

It is the equivalent of putting NHS equipment in a pawn shop.

(Crazy things go on when PFI and PPP are about: a hospital was selling its equipment to a private medical company.)

Chapter 6

Rosie Kane, SSP List MSP for Glasgow

Just like Colin and Carolyn, Rosie has blazed a trail since being elected in 2003. Her star is still on the ascendancy. If Tommy Sheridan's clenched fist of defiance was the defining image of the swearing in ceremony at the opening of the Parliament in 1999, Rosie's hand-written proclamation on the palm of her hand, stating 'My oath is to the people', was the essential and iconic representation of the new rainbow Parliament in 2003. She was lambasted for wearing casual attire in the Parliament, particularly at the swearing in ceremony, for promising to bring colour, imagination, diversity and attitude into the Parliament and variously designated leader of the Toytown Revolutionary Front and the Play School Tendency. The crescendo of abuse climaxed with her attempts to persuade politicians to stop using the term 'ned' to describe young, working class kids.

However, others applauded Rosie for her down-to-earth, refreshingly direct and breezily subversive style. And some even congratulated Rosie on her exuberance and energy in trying to bring the politics of the street into the Parliamentary chamber. These plaudits rang true with her frank admissions over the cause of her previous agoraphobia (a sexual attack) and an on-going battle with clinical depression and her big-heartedness in putting up asylum seeker Mercy Okolo and her daughter, Perieliz, in her two-bedroomed flat for nearly six months, and fund-raising for the Scotland team in the Homeless World Cup.

For these reasons of infamy, Rosie won the 'one-to-watch' category in the *Herald*/Zurich insurance annual Politician of the Year awards in 2003 and the *Scotsman Guide to Scottish Politics* commented that she has 'a gallus genius for publicity and has even overshadowed her colleague Tommy Sheridan'. Meanwhile the *Holyrood* magazine believed she had 'the look and swagger of a ringleader', the *Herald* believed she could blether for Scotland and the *Daily Mail* remarked that the book, the *Wit and Wisdom of Rosie Kane*, would not be far off.

Generator of as many column inches as Tommy Sheridan, she writes a column in the *Sunday Mail*, has been a columnist for *Scottish Socialist Voice* and appeared in the *Vagina Monologues* and must be one of the few MSPs to be able to boast that she has appeared on North Korean television.

After a year in Parliament, the former *Scotsman* Parliamentary Sketch Writer, Robert McNeil, commented of Rosie:

A fish out of water. We all had high hopes for her, with her amusing outfits and her big smile. Oh, with what glee did we anticipate this daring experiment of bringing the language and clothing of the streets to the starchy tedium of the chamber. She could have taken them on. She could have ripped through the hypocrisy. She could have felled them with one slap of her be-sloganed palm. But they defeated her. Perhaps she has one last burst of mayhem left. (3/5) (Scotsman 3 May 2004)

After returning from her period of sick leave to deal with her depression, there seems plenty of life left in the comeback kid. The counterpart to taking in the Ikolos was Rosie's adoption of the pet rat of deported child asylum seeker, Alex Gulshan Babayeva from Azerbaijan. Her point was that the pet rat, Maxi, although taken in by animal protection agency, the SSPCA, had more rights than its owner, a human being. This was no small feat given Rosie's dislike of rodents.

Again, the assessment of the *Scottish Socialist Voice* (9 July 2004) of Rosie's first year was rather different from that of the *Scotsman*:

Rosie has played a key part in turning the question of asylum and immigration into a human rights issue in Scotland in the past year. Her protests against Dungavel and her support for the Ay family and Mercy Ikolo took on Europe-wide proportions when she followed the deported Ays to Berlin, in August of last year. Though Rosie had to take a well-publicised break from work at the beginning of 2004, she has returned with renewed vigour and enthusiasm, taking up issues around the stigmatisation of people with mental health problems. Rosie continues to campaign against the proposed extension to the M74 motorway and is promoting and supporting the Scottish Homeless World Cup team.

Political Inspiration

Rosie ascribes her later political coming of age to the opening up of space in her life after divorce and upon entering higher education. A trip to visit her mum led her to bump into environmental protestors living in the trees in the Pollok Free State. This process allowed her to make connections between environmental degradation, her awareness of deprivation experienced, and seen around her, during her childhood, as well as concern about developments in world events and knowledge of her grandmother's encounters with poor relief. These strands came together for her in becoming a socialist.

Leisure and Pastime Interests

Writing poems and stories, a variety of music (including the Mamas and Papas, Snow Patrol and Franz Ferdinand), soap operas, occasional marathons. She has an ambition to write a play. As of 2004, this list also includes football as well as following and supporting the Scotland team in the Homeless World Cup. Political opponents should note she has a brown belt in karate.

Biography

Born 1961, Glasgow. Politically came alive in 1995 after being involved in the campaign to oppose the extension of the M74 through Pollok, known as the Pollok Free State. This political dawning led her to join the Scottish Socialist Alliance, the forerunner of the SSP, in the same year. Her environmental campaigning continued with the battle against the extension of the M77. She became a youth worker in Drumchapel, Glasgow. She lives in Glasgow with her two daughters, Susanne, aged 16, and Nicola, aged 19.

The Revolutionary Witticisms of Rosie Kane

New Advances in Medical Knowledge

(Dr Kane pronounces on the problem of those agitators who spurn the use of megaphones and prefer shouting):

I've got socialist throat.

(Rosie and Tommy were both afflicted by laryngitis)

On Being a Working Class Thief

(During the 2003 Scottish Parliament election campaign, SNP MSP Kenny Gibson referred to the young kids in Pollok as the 'thieves of Pollok'. At the election night count, where she was elected, Rosie retorted):

I must be one of the thieves Kenny has been talking about because I've just stolen his seat.

If Music be the Food of Life …

If protest was opera, I would be Pavarotti.

On the Economics of Motorways...

> If the construction of a massive road was the remedy for unemployment and poverty, I would be out there building one myself.

Her Red-Green Feminist Campaigning Slogan for the 1999 Scottish Parliament Elections

> Save the world ... and to hell with the washing up!

On Reading the Work of the Great Leader

> I bought it out of kindness. When I ended up in jail overnight, I had nothing else with me and I read it.

(Tommy Sheridan and Alan McCombes wrote *Imagine: A Socialist Vision for the Twenty-First Century*.)

On Being Asked if Tommy Sheridan is the Most Attractive of the Party Leaders

> Uuuugh, he's like a brother. Even thinking about it would be an arrestable offence.

A Spot of Difficulty Over Lunch

(Following the colourful objections of Labour MSP Rhona Brankin about Carolyn and Rosie bringing some striking nursery nurses into Parliament for lunch after their demonstration and causing a queue for food):

> She was like a bloody Tasmanian devil. ... She

should bring in a packed lunch [next time] and give us all a break.

(Rhona then became known by her nickname, 'Huffy'.)

Everything is Political, Politics is Everywhere

(Being interviewed in a bar and picking up a nacho):

I mean I could get political about these nachos. ... Maybe they're genetically modified. I could get political about anything.

On Her First Day in Parliament at the Mound

Like Westminster with MFI furniture.

And Learning How to Operate in Parliament

I'm learning the lingo at the moment. It's sounds like a toilet thing – I like to have a motion every day.

On Being 'Double Trouble' Alongside Fellow Glasgow SSP List MSP, Tommy Sheridan

We're Mr and Mrs Socialism!

Dealing With Political Foes

(Responding to tormentor SNP MSP Stewart Stevenson):

This is supposed to be a poverty debate: you clearly have a poverty of decency!

On Returning to Parliament with Mixed Metaphors

> The danger is running before I can walk, so I need just to be careful. But I climbed a mountain today so I'm really pleased with myself.

On Why She Had to Return to the Political Fray

> There is a limit to the time any person can stand another day of Fern Brittan and Philip Schofield on the telly.

Admitting She Knows Little about Marx, Lenin and Trotsky...

(Where her political credo comes from):

> It starts at my toes, travels up my body and comes out my mouth.

... But that Her Politics Do Come from Somewhere

> Everyone should climb a tree once in the their life. It's quite an emotional experience. You're never the same again.

Giving Advice to Labour MSP Backbenchers

> Prison's a state of mind. You get out of yours!

(On a debate on asylum rights.)

Asking a Lot of Other MSPs

> I ask members to imagine something for a minute –

when people are in prison, they use their imagination to survive. I ask everyone in this chamber to imagine that they are not MSPs or ministers, to forget about the Executive and to pretend, for a minute, that they are human beings.

(On the same debate about asylum rights.)

Describing Labour Women aka Blair's Babes

They're all wee Ally McBeals with perfect hair.

Trying to Avoid Arrest at Faslane

(To the police):

We are the inspectors of the weapons of mass destruction and we know where they are!

On Priorities in Life

My kitchen has an unused cooker but an often-touched Che poster.

Parents Fuck You Up (Larkin)

(On her parents, sex and appearing in the *Vagina Monologues*):

My parents don't talk about the pants', department. ... My dad's not getting to go. I don't think he knows the word vagina or monologue and I'm keeping it that way. I've told him the [Edinburgh] Playhouse is up a hill and it would not be good for him to go. My mum will be going but I think she thinks vagina is a heart problem and confuses it with angina.

If Anyone from Her Day Job Turned Up at the Playhouse

I might just call them a bunch of vaginas if they try to heckle. I've been dying to say that to a few of them.

Discussing the Differences Between Audiences in Glasgow and Edinburgh

(Rosie intended to tell the audiences in Edinburgh attending the *Vagina Monologues*):

You'll have had your jokes then!

(Modern Weegie adaptation of the well-worn Edinburgh Morningside refrain 'You'll have had your tea then').

On Relations with Her Daughters

(As a long time vegetarian and environmental campaigner):

I had to buy them Big Macs the other day. They're just poor victims of capitalism, really.

On the New David Beckham of 2004: Wayne Rooney

I'll tell you what I noticed about him was his red hair,

red nose, freckles and peely-wally legs. All of which can mean only one thing. Young Wayne is on the wrong side and his genes are screaming out for a place in the Scotland team.

(This was before his ill-advised interview with *The Sun*.)

Remembering Her School Days and Celebrating the Last Day of Term in Parliament in the Old Building

I just feel like bringing in my Kerplunk!

(The children's game Kerplunk was as emblematic of the 1970s as Chopper bicycles and the Bay City Rollers.)

On the Scurrilous Rumour that Gail Sheridan, Partner of Tommy Sheridan, had had Cosmetic Plastic Surgery

Aye, she's had plastic surgery, plastic surgery to get Tommy off her back.

Questioning the Ability of Custodial Security Firm, Reliance, to Manage the Electronic Tagging Operation

No doubt the satellite will get lost, and the tags will be made of Plasticine and Sellotape. Maybe, the satellites will be made from Fairy Liquid bottles.

(Reliance had developed a habit of losing prisoners and wrongly letting them go.)

On the Then Scottish Finance Minister's Caring, Sharing Side of His Character

(Following the announcement of huge job losses in the central and devolved civil service by Gordon Brown, no one could be found to say what this meant for the devolved Scottish civil servants):

> Where was Scottish Finance Minister Andy Kerr? Out of the country. Andy Disnae Kerr more like.

Having a Useful Football Epiphany at the Homeless World Cup, Gothenburg

> I didn't even like football before I came here. … It's opened my eyes, added a new string to my political bow and given me new things to take back to the Scottish Parliament. I think I'll be a better politician because of it.

Taking Her Daughters to See Shakespeare at the Theatre

> All was going well until my eldest, Nicola, asked me a question about one of the characters. In a tiny and respectful whisper, I replied. At that point, the geezer in front unravelled himself in all his pomposity and told us to do our talking after the performance. He totally peeped the weans' gas and the wee souls just sat clutching their IrnBru cans, looking oppressed. I was livid, as all my work in persuading them that Shakey was the act for them had been blasted by this purist. 'Is this a plonker I see before me?' I whispered to Nicola. Leaving the theatre, I buttonholed Mr

Intensity and told him: 'My daughter was seeking guidance, which I gave her. You, however, need patience and understanding. Seek it yourself.'

Viva Shakey and Che

Che-kspeare: Shakey and Che as my ideal man.

Getting Ready for the New Building at Holyrood

That's it, we're out on our ears in MSP-land. ... I am a wee bit worried about how the new Holyrood building looks. I am not an architect but I know what I like and I think that from certain angles, our new big hoose looks like the council swimming baths. I'd better take my water wings just in case I dive in at the deep end ... again.

Of Gooses, Ganders and Sauces in Parliament

When Gordon Brown was asked how much he was prepared to spend on war [in Iraq], he replied that he would spend as much as it takes. That is the 'Brown principle'. I ask members to imagine what would happen if that principle could be applied to poverty.

Being Nice Does Not Always Win

Rosie Kane: Will the member give way?

Labour MSP Christine May: No. This is my maiden speech.

Rosie Kane: It will be an easy question.
Labour MSP Christine May: No. I am not giving way.

In Health and in Sickness …

So Jack McConnell wants to ban smoking in public places. Good on him. But if the First Minister sticks to his guns, he'll have to close down Glasgow. Walking around the city is apparently the equivalent of smoking 40 fags a day. Maybe Jack thinks this pollution is caused by the expelled smokers having a puff outside their workplace. But traffic is the real culprit.

Stoical in Defeat?

(On explaining what use she would put the M74 extension to):

It's gonna be 50ft high so at least it will make a good shelter for the homeless.

On Her Overnight Accommodation at the European Social Forum in London

There's no place quite like the Dome but there's no place like home, either. But, then, maybe I couldn't appreciate it because I'm not a Londoner.

Chapter 7
Afterword

I have enjoyed putting together this short collection of Colin, Carolyn and Rosie's witticisms. The humour and feistiness of their witticisms helped make the onerous task of searching out their many and varied warblings and feats of verbal gymnastics, throughout the thousands of press reports about them, amusing and worthwhile. In particular, I would like to thank Colin for his efforts in recording many of his previously unrecorded witticisms. I am also grateful to the diarists and journalists of various newspapers like the *Herald, Scotsman, Sunday Mail, Edinburgh Evening News* and *Glasgow Evening Times* for often recording the warblings of the three MSPs, and to the official record of the Scottish Parliament for transcribing verbatim the debates and exchanges in the chamber.

Ken Smith and David Belcher, the *Herald*'s diarists, commented that 'Politicians are usually unconscious comedians – but only when they are trying to be serious' (*Herald* 7 October 2004). The three MSPs buck this trend: they are consciously humorous for serious purposes. The evidence of their witticisms presented here goes a long way to invalidating the 'all socialists are serious bores' thesis of the *News of the World* (20 June 2004), when it recommended:

All [SSP] members to contribute towards the purchase of a sense of humour. This will be shared among elected members, each using it for a day at a time. Comrade Sheridan asks to be exempted. He is not joking. Carolyn Leckie will also make her own arrangements.

To paraphrase Lenin, were these revolutionary left-wing witticisms an infantile disorder? Being able to think on one's feet with witty repartee and ripostes is not easy, especially when under attack from political foes. It indicates a large degree of deftness and surefootedness. This suggests that there is nothing overly infantile about Colin, Carolyn and Rosie's witticisms. Rather, it suggests a level of intelligence and maturity. None of them show any tendency to become formulaic and predictable in their witticisms. Having a sense of humour is another valuable commodity in the goldfish bowl of Holyrood, the Scottish media and the central belt of Scotland. But humour imbued with socialist political intent makes this an even more valuable commodity.

So, of course, some politicians and partisan commentators have made out Colin, Carolyn and Rosie's witticisms to be infantile, ridiculous, irresponsible and outrageous. This is par for the course. But that the witticisms have been effective in helping to achieve what they sought to do, and because this has been recognised and commented upon by others outside the ranks of the SSP, suggests that Lenin's question can be answered with a firm negative.

With their witticisms set down on paper in one place

for now and recorded for posterity for ever more, I look forward to the task of producing an updated and revised edition once the three musketeers have passed more comments, observations and treatises on the state of Scotland and the world and how to put both right. The third sitting of the Scottish Parliament begins in 2007. I'm sure that Colin, Carolyn and Rosie will be there to carry on their good work and revolutionary witticisms.